MW01099077

Land of Liberty

Wyoming

by Kim Covert

Consultant:
Carl V. Hallberg
Reference Archivist
Wyoming State Archives

Capstone
press

Mankato, Minnesota

Capstone Press
151 Good Counsel Drive • P.O. Box 669 • Mankato, Minnesota 56002
http://www.capstone-press.com

Library of Congress Cataloging-in-Publication Data
Covert, Kim.
    Wyoming / by Kim Covert.
    p. cm.—(Land of liberty)
    Includes bibliographical references (p. 61) and index.
    Contents: About Wyoming—Land, climate, and wildlife—History of
Wyoming—Government and Politics—Economy and Resources—People and
Culture—Recipe—Flag and seal—Almanac—Timeline—Words to Know.
    ISBN 0-7368-2207-0 (hardcover)
    1. Wyoming—Juvenile literature. [1. Wyoming.] I. Title. II. Series.
F761.3.C69 2004
978.7—dc21   2002154712

Summary: An introduction to the geography, history, government, politics,
    economy, resources, people, and culture of Wyoming, including maps,
    charts, and a recipe.

Editorial Credits
Rebecca Glaser, editor; Jennifer Schonborn, series designer; Linda Clavel, book
    designer; Enoch Peterson, illustrator; Alta Schaffer and Kelly Garvin, photo
    researchers; Eric Kudalis, product planning editor

Photo Credits
Cover images: Cattle drive in northern Wyoming, Houserstock/M.L. Abbott;
Snake River with Grand Tetons in background, Digital Vision

American Buildings Survey/Historic American Engineering Record, 24; Capstone
Press/Gary Sundermeyer, 54; Cheryl R. Richter, 43, 57; Corbis, 26; Corbis/Bill
Ross, 38; Corbis/Owen Franken, 48; The Denver Public Library, 16; Digital
Vision/Gerry Ellis, 56; Grand Teton Music Festival, 52; Houserstock/Dave G.
Houser, 12, 30, 50–51; Houserstock/Susan Kaye, 14–15, 42; Houserstock/Steve
Bly, 46; Library of Congress, 34, 58; Jeff Henry/Roche Jaune Pictures Inc., 40,
44–45, 63; John Elk III, 8; Mai/Timepix, 37; One Mile Up Inc., 55 (both);
PhotoDisc Inc., 1, 4; Stock Montage Inc., 18, 23; U.S. Postal Service, 59; Visuals
Unlimited/Inga Spence, 28–29; Wyoming Division of Cultural Resources, 20

Artistic Effects
PhotoDisc Inc., Digital Vision

1 2 3 4 5 6 08 07 06 05 04 03

Table of Contents

The geyser Old Faithful in Yellowstone National Park erupts nearly every hour.

Chapter 1

About Wyoming

Almost every hour in Yellowstone National Park, a geyser shoots hot water higher than 100 feet (30 meters) into the air. Millions of people visit the northwest corner of Wyoming each year to see this geyser, Old Faithful.

Heat and pressure underground create Yellowstone's geysers and other thermal features. An ancient volcanic basin under Yellowstone heats up rock areas. The hot rock boils water underground. When heat and pressure forces water above ground, thermal features are created. Besides geysers, the park has hot springs, pools of boiling water, and bubbling mud pools.

The thermal features and scenery interested early explorers. People wanted to set aside the area as a park. They did not want

to let settlers or private businesses claim the land. In 1872, Yellowstone National Park became the first national park in the world.

The Cowboy State

Wyoming is often called the Cowboy State. In the late 1800s, cowboys herded cattle on Wyoming's open ranges. Fewer cowboys live in the state today, but many Wyomingites still admire the cowboy way of life.

The Equality State is another nickname for Wyoming. In 1869, Wyoming Territory passed a law allowing women to vote. It was the first place in the nation where women had equal voting rights.

Wyoming is located in the northwestern United States. Covering 97,914 square miles (253,597 square kilometers), it is the 10th largest state. Six states border Wyoming. Montana borders it on the north and northwest. South Dakota and Nebraska border Wyoming on the east. Colorado borders Wyoming to the south, and Utah lies to the southwest. Idaho lies along Wyoming's western border.

Wyoming Cities

MONTANA

IDAHO

SOUTH DAKOTA

NEBRASKA

Sheridan •

Cody •

Gillette •

Newcastle •

Wind River
American Indian
Reservation

• Jackson

Casper •

WYOMING

Green River • • Rock Springs

Laramie •

Cheyenne

UTAH

COLORADO

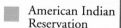

Legend

	American Indian Reservation
★	Capital
•	City

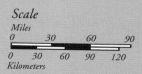

N
W   E
S

Scale
Miles
0   30   60   90

0   30   60   90   120
Kilometers

7

Jackson Lake is nestled between the mountains of the Teton Range.

Chapter 2

Land, Climate, and Wildlife

The Continental Divide runs crosswise through Wyoming along a ridge of mountains. This imaginary line splits North America into two parts. Rivers east of the Continental Divide flow toward the Atlantic Ocean. Rivers west of this line flow toward the Pacific Ocean.

Wyoming's land features divide the state into three regions. The Great Plains are in the east and the Rocky Mountains are in the west. The Intermontane Basins lie between the mountains.

The Great Plains

The Great Plains covers much of central North America. The western edge of the Great Plains extends into eastern Wyoming. More than 150 types of grasses cover the plains. The grasses make the area good for grazing sheep and cattle. Sagebrush, a type of shrub, grows well on the dry plains. Cottonwood, blue spruce, and willow trees grow along streams and rivers in the plains.

Parts of the Black Hills rise above Wyoming's northeastern plains. Ponderosa pines grow on the hills. These trees make the hills look black from a distance. Wyoming's lowest point is in the Black Hills. It is 3,100 feet (945 meters) above sea level.

The Rocky Mountains

The Rocky Mountains cover much of Wyoming. Several mountain ranges make up the Rocky Mountains. Gannett Peak in the Wind River Range is the highest point in Wyoming. It is 13,804 feet (4,207 meters) above sea level.

Forests cover about one-fifth of Wyoming. Most of the forests grow in the mountain regions. Lodgepole pine, Douglas fir, and Engleman spruce trees grow in the forests. The state

Wyoming's Land Features

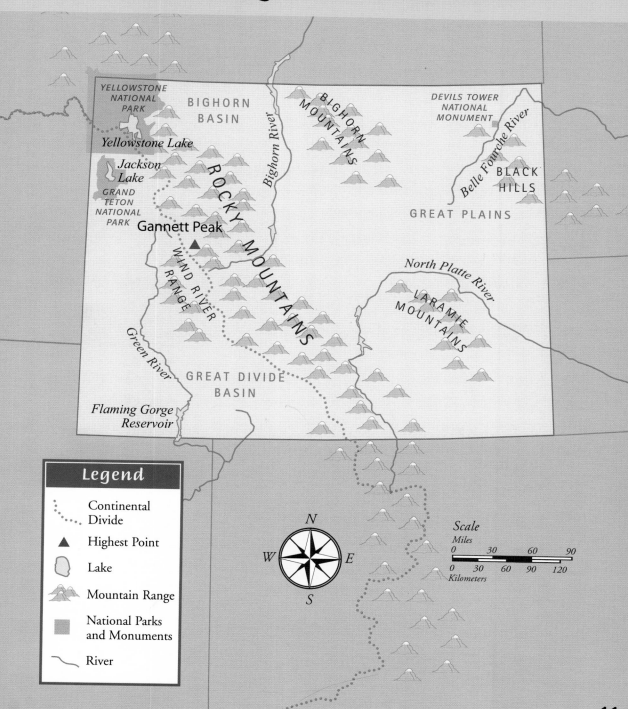

YELLOWSTONE NATIONAL PARK

BIGHORN BASIN

Yellowstone Lake

Jackson Lake

GRAND TETON NATIONAL PARK

Gannett Peak

ROCKY MOUNTAINS

WIND RIVER RANGE

Bighorn River

BIGHORN MOUNTAINS

DEVILS TOWER NATIONAL MONUMENT

Belle Fourche River

BLACK HILLS

GREAT PLAINS

North Platte River

LARAMIE MOUNTAINS

Green River

GREAT DIVIDE BASIN

Flaming Gorge Reservoir

Legend

- .... Continental Divide
- ▲ Highest Point
- Lake
- Mountain Range
- National Parks and Monuments
- River

N
W E
S

Scale

Miles
0   30   60   90

0   30   60   90   120
Kilometers

11

Devils Tower

In northeastern Wyoming, a gigantic rock rises 1,267 feet (386 meters) above the ground. Known as Devils Tower, this rock's origin has proved to be a mystery. Wind and water probably helped form it.

In 1906, President Theodore Roosevelt proclaimed Devils Tower as the first national monument in the United States. Thousands of people visit each year. Some people climb the rock's high, straight walls. In 1977, a few scenes in *Close Encounters of the Third Kind* were filmed at Devils Tower. This movie helped make Devils Tower famous.

has four national forests. Medicine Bow National Forest is in southern Wyoming. Shoshone and Bighorn are national forests in northern Wyoming. Bridger-Teton National Forest covers the Rocky Mountains in the west.

Wyoming's largest lakes are in the mountain regions. The state's largest natural lake is Yellowstone Lake, located in Yellowstone National Park. Jackson Lake, the second largest lake in the state, lies in the Teton Range.

The Intermontane Basins

The Intermontane Basins are low, flat lands between Wyoming's mountain ranges. The basin areas are also called holes. They contain deep canyons carved by streams and rivers. Short grasses cover the Intermontane Basins. Sheep and cattle graze on the grasses. Few trees grow there.

The Great Divide Basin, one of the largest Intermontane Basins, is in southern Wyoming. It is one of the driest areas in the United States. People call the Great Divide Basin the Red Desert because of its sand dunes and red, rocky land. Plants in the basin include sagebrush, yucca, and cactus.

Climate

Wyoming's temperatures vary with land elevation. In mountain areas, the temperature averages 59 degrees Fahrenheit (15 degrees Celsius) in July. On the plains, the average July temperature is 71 degrees Fahrenheit (22 degrees Celsius).

Precipitation also varies throughout the state. The high mountain areas can receive more than 45 inches (114 centimeters) of precipitation each year. Heavy snow falls in the winter. In the Bighorn Basin, as little as 5 inches (13 centimeters) of rain falls each year.

Wildlife

Wyoming is home to a variety of wildlife. Moose, bighorn sheep, grizzly bears, and mountain lions live in the state. Smaller mammals include the fox, mink, coyote, bobcat, and jackrabbit. Bald eagles and golden eagles nest in Wyoming.

The largest elk herd in the United States spends each winter in Jackson Hole. In 1912, Wyoming's National Elk

Refuge was created near Jackson. Each winter, the refuge provides food and protection to more than 7,500 elk.

Some animals in Wyoming are endangered. The state has passed laws against hunting or killing them because they may die out completely. Wyoming's endangered animals include the whooping crane and the black-footed ferret.

In the early 1990s, the gray wolf was endangered. In 1995, park officials released gray wolves in Yellowstone National Park. The program was successful. In 2003, the gray wolf was removed from the endangered species list.

The National Elk Refuge north of Jackson is home to herds of elk from October to May. In summer, the elk migrate back to higher lands in Wyoming's mountains.

The Shoshone lived in the Wyoming area in the 1800s. By 1884, when this picture was taken, the Shoshone lived on a reservation.

Chapter 3

History of Wyoming

Around 1800, several American Indian groups lived in Wyoming. They included the Shoshone, Crow, Sioux, Cheyenne, and Arapaho people. Many Indians came from the east as white settlers took their land. The Indians lived in small groups of about 100 people. They followed bison herds on the plains of eastern Wyoming.

Mountain Men

John Colter was the first white man known to explore Wyoming. He explored the area in 1807. Colter wrote about steaming geysers and huge waterfalls. He probably was in an area near present-day Yellowstone National Park.

In the early 1800s, American mountain men entered Wyoming to explore and to trap beavers. They sold beaver pelts to people in Europe who made hats and coats from these furs. Kit Carson, Jim Bridger, Davey Jackson, and Jedediah Smith were the first mountain men in Wyoming. In the 1820s and 1830s, fur trade was the main business in Wyoming. Fur traders exchanged pelts for guns, compasses, and other tools.

Early trappers in Wyoming did not set up trading posts or forts. In 1825, they began meeting once each year to exchange goods and get new supplies. They called these meetings

Jim Bridger was one of the first mountain men to explore the Wyoming area.

rendezvous (ron-DEH-voo). At a rendezvous, the trappers traded with American Indians, held feasts, played games, and danced. They held the last rendezvous in 1840. By then, very few beavers were left to trap.

The Way West

In the mid-1800s, many people began passing through Wyoming on their way to Oregon. Oregon's rich farmland attracted many people from the eastern United States. In 1812, Robert Stuart and a group of men had found South Pass in southwestern Wyoming. This low place in the Wind River Range allowed wagons to travel easily across the mountains. South Pass later became part of the Oregon Trail.

Other routes west crossed through Wyoming. In 1847, a religious group called the Mormons made a trail to Salt Lake City, Utah. Their road became known as the Mormon Trail. Some settlers turned off the Oregon Trail toward California. Thousands of settlers followed this California Trail during the 1849 gold rush. Other pioneers traveled the Bozeman Trail,

Settlers on the Oregon Trail often traveled in wagon trains for safety. At night, they circled their wagons for protection from possible attacks by Indians.

which opened in 1864. The Bozeman Trail cut across northeastern Wyoming. It led to gold mines in Montana.

The U.S. Army built forts in Wyoming to protect pioneers as they moved west. Fort Bridger was established in southwestern Wyoming. Soldiers built Fort Phil Kearny along the Bozeman Trail. Fort Laramie in southeastern Wyoming became the most important western military post. Travelers stopped there to rest and buy supplies.

"The white man, who possesses this whole vast country from sea to sea . . . cannot know the cramp we feel in this little spot, with the underlying remembrance of the fact . . . that every foot of what you proudly call America not very long ago belonged to the red man . . . "
—Chief Washakie, Shoshone Nation

Conflicts

Early settlers had many conflicts with American Indian tribes. The settlers often killed animals that the Indians needed for food. The American Indians did not want forts built on their hunting grounds. They sometimes attacked soldiers and settlers along the trails.

American Indians and white people fought many battles. Fort Phil Kearny in northern Wyoming had the bloodiest history of any fort in the West. This fort was the site of many battles between the U.S. government and the Cheyenne, Sioux, and Arapaho Indians. In one battle, all 81 soldiers at the fort were killed.

American Indians signed several treaties with the United States. In 1868, American Indians and the U.S. government signed the Fort Laramie Treaty. They agreed to close the Bozeman Trail and Fort Phil Kearny. In return, American Indians allowed the government to build railroads across

southern Wyoming. In 1868, the Fort Bridger Treaty established the Wind River Reservation for the Shoshone. Chief Washakie was their leader. In 1877, Chief Washakie agreed to allow Arapaho tribes to share the reservation. The Arapaho were longtime enemies of the Shoshone.

The Wyoming Territory

In 1861, Wyoming became part of the Dakota Territory, which included the land that is now North Dakota, South Dakota, and Montana. On July 25, 1868, the U.S. Congress separated the Wyoming area into the Wyoming Territory. Cheyenne became its capital.

In 1868, the Union Pacific Railroad was completed across southern Wyoming Territory. Many towns were built along the tracks, including Laramie, Rawlins, Rock Springs, Green River, and Evanston. People came from the eastern United States. They worked on the railroad, bought land, and opened businesses.

In 1869, women voted in Wyoming Territory. It was the first place to give women the right to vote.

In 1869, Wyoming Territory passed a law that gave women the right to vote. Women could not vote anywhere else in the nation. Lawmakers hoped that the new law would attract more women to Wyoming.

Statehood and Growth

Between 1880 and 1890, the population of Wyoming had increased from 20,789 to 62,555. On July 10, 1890, Wyoming became the 44th state of the Union. The capital stayed at Cheyenne.

Many businesses grew over the next 30 years. Cattle ranching was a big business in northern Wyoming. By the early 1900s, coal mining was a major industry in Wyoming.

Completed in 1910, the Buffalo Bill Dam on the Shoshone River irrigates the land near Cody and Powell in the Bighorn Basin.

"The admission of the States of Wyoming and Idaho to the Union are events full of interest and congratulation . . . Another belt of States stretches from the Atlantic to the Pacific."

—U.S. President Benjamin Harrison, 1890

Because Wyoming has a dry climate, irrigation systems were built to bring water to dry farmlands. In 1905, the U.S. Reclamation Service began building the Buffalo Bill Dam in Wyoming. The dam was completed in 1910.

The oil industry also developed. The state's first oil well began production at Dallas Field in 1883. During the next 20 years, oil was discovered throughout northern and eastern Wyoming. Towns including Casper, Glenrock, and Newcastle grew because of nearby oil discoveries. The state's first oil refinery was built in Casper in 1894. This factory cleaned and made the oil into gasoline and other products. As demand for oil increased, large companies set up businesses in the state. By the mid-1920s, the state ranked fourth in the production of crude oil.

Economic Depression

In the 1920s, Wyomingites faced hard times. Farm prices dropped, many mines closed, and oil production decreased.

The Civilian Conservation Corps (CCC) was part of the New Deal during the Great Depression. This CCC camp was in the Bighorn National Forest.

A drought began in 1926 and continued well into the 1930s. The lack of water dried up large areas of farmland.

Factories and mines closed all over the United States during the Great Depression (1929–1939). The prices for cattle and sheep went down. The demand for coal and oil decreased. Many Wyomingites and others throughout the United States lost their jobs.

The U.S. government started programs to help people who had lost their jobs. President Franklin D. Roosevelt called these programs the New Deal. Workers for the Civilian Conservation Corps built dams, planted trees, and fought forest fires. Many Wyomingites worked to build dams in the state for irrigation.

War and Natural Resources

In 1941, the United States entered World War II (1939–1945). Some Wyomingites were soldiers. The U.S. military used Wyoming's coal and oil for fuel. Wyoming's cattle ranchers supplied soldiers with meat.

World War II created demand for Wyoming's natural resources. Major oil discoveries were made in northeastern Wyoming. By the end of the war, about 25 refineries were operating in the state. During the war, Wyoming's coal mines produced 9 million tons (8 million metric tons) of coal per year. After the war, mineral production became the state's most important industry.

Industry Brings Growth

Wyoming's oil resources continued to develop in the 1950s and 1960s. A pipeline built through the Green River Basin in 1955 carried oil. In the 1970s, oil prices were very high. Businesses looked for new oil fields throughout Wyoming. New fields were found in southwestern Wyoming and in the Powder River Basin in northeastern Wyoming.

The state's energy industry brought more workers to the state. From 1970 to 1980, Wyoming's population increased by more than 41 percent. The state produced energy for other parts of the country. Its oil, coal, and uranium businesses grew. Uranium is a silver-white radioactive metal that is the main source of nuclear energy.

By the 1980s, other countries produced cheaper oil and uranium. The prices for Wyoming's coal and oil dropped. Many Wyoming mines and oil wells closed. Workers lost their jobs and moved away from the state.

In the 1990s, Wyoming's population started growing again. Low-sulfur coal mines opened, bringing jobs to the state. Low-sulfur coal produces less pollution when it burns than other coal does. Wyoming also increased its production of natural gas. Natural gas is used in vehicles and to heat homes. The state's population grew almost 9 percent from 1990 to 2000.

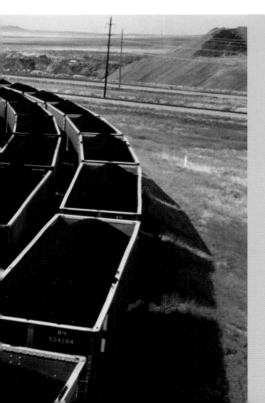

Train cars called gondolas carry coal from a surface coal mine in Wyoming.

Completed in 1888, Wyoming's capitol was built from sandstone granite. Most of this stone came from Wyoming.

Chapter 4

Government and Politics

Wyoming adopted its state constitution in 1890. It has been amended several times. Two-thirds of the state legislature and a majority of the state's voters must approve changes to the constitution.

In 1968, an amendment allowed citizens to propose, or initiate, a new law. If a person gathers enough signatures in support, the law will be put on a ballot. If 50 percent of voters approve the law, it goes into effect.

Branches of Government

Wyoming's government has executive, legislative, and judicial branches. The executive branch makes sure laws are followed.

The governor heads the executive branch. Citizens elect each governor for a four-year term. Wyoming has no lieutenant governor. If a governor dies, the secretary of state serves as the governor. Voters select a new governor in the next election.

Two groups in the state legislature work to make the state's laws. Wyoming's senate has 30 members. The house of representatives has 60 members. Voters elect senators to four-year terms. Representatives serve two-year terms.

The judicial branch is Wyoming's court system. The supreme court is the highest court in the state. It consists of five justices who serve eight-year terms. The major trial courts in the state are the district courts. Judges at these courts serve six-year terms. Wyoming has 25 circuit courts. They handle civil cases that ask for damages of less than $7,000. Circuit courts also hear family violence cases. Each city has a municipal court, which hears cases about city laws.

Wyoming's State Government

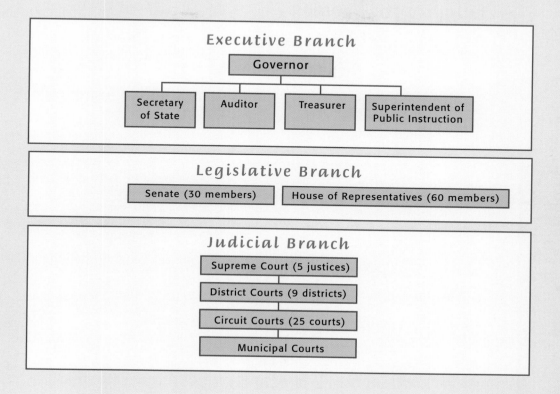

A nominating committee selects Supreme Court and district court justices. The committee chooses the names of three qualified lawyers. The governor selects one to serve on the Supreme Court until the next election. Then, voters can choose whether to keep this justice on the court.

Equality for Women

Wyoming was one of the earliest states to appoint women to positions in government. In 1870, Esther Hobart Morris became the nation's first woman to be appointed a justice of

Nellie Tayloe Ross was the first female governor in the United States. She finished her husband's term after he died in 1924.

"We must practice Wyoming's motto of 'The Equality State.' We must acknowledge each other's worth and dignity, or we will lose our basic values."

—Wyoming governor Jim Geringer, January 15, 1996

the peace. Her job was to listen to cases in local courts of law. She also could perform marriages.

In 1924, Wyoming citizens elected Nellie Tayloe Ross as their governor. Her husband, William Ross, had died that year. She was elected to finish her husband's term. Ross was the nation's first female state governor. She served from 1925 to 1927. In 1933, President Franklin Roosevelt appointed her as the first woman to head the U.S. Mint. She held this position for 20 years.

Politics

Wyoming is known for its conservative politics. Most of the state's elected officials have been Republicans. Members of the Republican political party think the federal government is too powerful. They want it to have a smaller role in state government. Republicans also believe in low taxes. Wyoming is one of the most Republican states in the country. More than half of its citizens are registered Republicans.

Wyoming Government Today

Wyoming has no state income tax. Citizens do not pay a portion of their income to the state. Businesses do not pay a tax on their profits. Low taxes help attract new businesses and people.

In Wyoming, much of the state government's money comes from a sales tax. People pay this tax on items they buy. In 2002, the government collected more than $515 million in sales tax. Wyoming has also collected a mineral severance tax since 1968. The state collects a percentage of the mining industry's profits.

Education is the biggest expense in Wyoming's budget. The state has to run small schools for students living in remote areas. But some children still must ride the bus 75 miles (121 kilometers) each way to school. For this reason, Wyoming allows 14-year-olds to get a driver's license. They are allowed to drive to school and back.

For many years, people have argued over control of Wyoming's land. Today, the federal government controls almost half of Wyoming's land. Most of this land is in national parks and forests. Some ranchers and mining businesses want the state to control more of its land.

Dick Cheney

Richard (Dick) Cheney was born on January 30, 1941, in Lincoln, Nebraska. As a boy, he moved with his family to Casper, Wyoming. He graduated from the University of Wyoming. In 1977, Wyoming voters elected Cheney to the U.S. House of Representatives. He held this position until 1989. That year, President George H. W. Bush named him U.S. secretary of defense.

Cheney directed U.S. operations against Iraq during the Gulf War (1991). The United States fought in this war with Iraq after Iraq's army invaded Kuwait in 1990. President Bush awarded Cheney the Presidential Medal of Freedom for his leadership.

In 2000, George W. Bush chose Cheney to be his vice presidential running mate. Bush and Cheney won the election by a close margin. In 2001, Cheney became the vice president of the United States.

They want businesses to expand on the land. But many Wyomingites want this land to remain under federal control. They want the areas to remain open for hunting, fishing, and hiking.

Wyoming is the number one coal producer in the nation.

Chapter 5

Economy and Resources

In the late 1900s and early 2000s, Wyoming has had a strong economy. Mining is the state's fastest-growing industry. Many Wyomingites work in service industries, including tourism, government, and transportation. Farming, ranching, and manufacturing are also part of Wyoming's economy.

Mining

Wyoming leads the nation in coal production. In 2001, 352 million tons (319 million metric tons) of coal were mined. The world's largest surface coal mine is near Gillette. This mine produces low-sulfur coal. Wyoming's coal is used to produce electricity in more than 20 states.

Wyoming also is the nation's leading producer of the minerals trona and bentonite. Trona is used mainly to produce glass products and baking soda. Sweetwater County has the largest known reserve of trona in the world. In 2001, Wyoming mined more than 18 million tons (16 million metric tons) of trona. Bentonite is mined in Crook County and in the Bighorn Basin. This claylike material is used in the production of oil, gas, cat litter, and cosmetics.

Other leading minerals include petroleum, natural gas, and uranium. Petroleum is used as a motor fuel and to make

A sunset highlights an oil well in Wyoming. Oil mined from wells in the state is used to make petroleum for motor fuel.

many products. The production of petroleum and petroleum products is centered in Casper. Wyoming's uranium was first discovered in 1949. Wyoming has the nation's second largest uranium deposits. The uranium from Wyoming mines is used to produce electricity.

In recent years, miners discovered rare platinum group metals in southeastern Wyoming. These metals are used in automobile parts and computer hard drives. They are also used in medicines to treat cancer and other illnesses. In the year 2000, the state government received about 2,000 new requests to build mines.

Service Industries

The federal government employs many Wyomingites. Some of them work in national forests and parks. Others work at Francis E. Warren Air Force Base near Cheyenne. The base provides jobs and money to the state. It also contains most of the nation's intercontinental ballistic missiles (ICBMs). These weapons can be launched from underground, rocket halfway around the world, and release nuclear warheads.

The government buried the United States' first ICBMs underground near Warren Air Force Base in 1958. The

Dude Ranches

Vacationers often visit Wyoming's dude ranches. A dude is someone who is unfamiliar with cowboy life. Visitors can ride horses and rope cattle at these ranches. Guests can stay for a few days or a few weeks. They may help work at the ranch.

government chose Wyoming because it was easy to build deep silos in the land. Many of the state's citizens wanted a strong military. But some people do not want ICBMs in Wyoming. They do not want Cheyenne to be a target of an enemy attack.

Wyoming's natural beauty attracts many visitors. The tourist industry began when Yellowstone National Park was founded in 1872. Today, about 3.5 million tourists visit Wyoming and spend about $1.5 billion each year. Winter sports, especially skiing, are becoming a major part of the tourist industry. Many Wyomingites have jobs in the tourism industry. They work as park rangers, ski patrol officers, resort owners, restaurant workers, and tour guides.

Agriculture

In 2000, about 9,200 ranches and farms were in Wyoming. The sale of cattle brings in most of the agricultural income. More than 1.5 million cattle graze on Wyoming land. Sheep are also important to the economy. Wyoming is second only to Texas in wool production.

Many of the crops raised in Wyoming are used to feed livestock. These crops include alfalfa, corn, and various

A park ranger in Yellowstone National Park teaches a group of children about the effects of forest fires.

meadow grasses. Other crops include sugar beets, barley, dry beans, and potatoes. Wyoming's growing season ranges between 90 and 120 days. Most farmers rely on irrigation to raise their crops. Dry farming in the Great Plains region produces wheat and barley. The dry farming method does not use irrigation.

Manufacturing

Manufacturing is not a big part of Wyoming's economy. Manufacturers in the state include chemical producers,

petroleum refineries, and food processors. They also include industrial machinery factories and wood product companies. Casper and Sinclair have large oil refineries. Factories in Torrington, Worland, and Lovell make sugar from sugar beets.

Some Wyomingites want to bring more industries into the state. They do not want Wyoming's economy to rely so heavily on the mineral industry. But many citizens are against increased manufacturing. They do not want too many people or businesses to move into the state. They enjoy living in a place that is quiet and uncrowded.

This cattle ranch is in the Wind River Valley west of Lander. Cattle ranching is the biggest part of agriculture in Wyoming.

In Wyoming, people can drive for hours on the highway and see very few cars.

Chapter 6

People and Culture

Wyoming has a great deal of land and the smallest population of any state. About 53,000 people live in Cheyenne, the largest city in Wyoming. Cheyenne would be a small city in many other states. Only five other cities have more than 15,000 people. They are Casper, Laramie, Rock Springs, Gillette, and Sheridan. Because of the small population, Wyoming has a low crime rate.

Ethnic Backgrounds

About 89 percent of Wyoming's residents have European backgrounds. Many of their ancestors came from Norway, Sweden, Denmark, Italy, and Germany. Hispanics represent

6.4 percent of the population. American Indians make up 2.1 percent of the state's total population. Many of them live on the Wind River Reservation in west central Wyoming. The reservation is the home of the Shoshone and Arapaho tribes. African Americans and Asians each make up less than one percent of the population.

A cowboy wrestles a steer at the Cheyenne Frontier Days Rodeo.

Wyoming's Ethnic Backgrounds

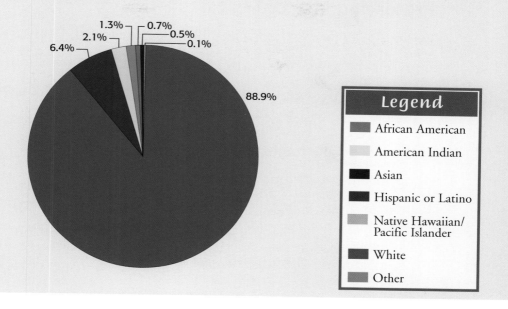

1.3% 0.7%
2.1% 0.5%
6.4% 0.1%

88.9%

Legend
- African American
- American Indian
- Asian
- Hispanic or Latino
- Native Hawaiian/ Pacific Islander
- White
- Other

Rodeos

During summer, at least one rodeo per week takes place in Wyoming. This traditional contest of cowboy skills includes events like bronc riding, steer wrestling, and cattle roping. In bull riding, contestants try to remain on a bucking bull for eight seconds.

One of the oldest rodeos takes place during Cheyenne Frontier Days each July. Cheyenne has hosted this rodeo since 1897. The 10-day celebration also features chili feasts and traditional Shoshone dancing, storytelling, and crafts.

Preserving the Old West

In 1896, the famous scout and hunter Buffalo Bill Cody founded the town of Cody. He organized a live show about life in Wyoming's early days. Around 1900, Buffalo Bill took his Wild West Show to Europe. Cowboys, American Indians, and other people important to America's West performed. Today, visitors can tour museums at the Buffalo Bill Historical Center in Cody. Displays tell about Buffalo Bill and American Indians. Old Trail Town is a group of buildings from frontier times located on the edge of Cody.

Many historic sites from the Oregon Trail days can be seen in Wyoming. Fort Laramie National Historic Site is north of Cheyenne. In the 1840s, soldiers at this fort protected pioneers on the Oregon Trail. Today, visitors learn about frontier life at this site. North of Guernsey, visitors can still see the ruts made by the pioneers' wagon wheels. These ruts are more than 100 years old. Independence Rock is west of Guernsey. More than 50,000 travelers on the Oregon Trail carved their names into this rock. Over the years, many names have worn away. Some names remain for visitors to see.

Visitors can tour frontier buildings at Old Trail Town in Cody. Famous outlaws Butch Cassidy and the Sundance Kid lived in one of the cabins in the 1800s.

Arts and Culture

Not all events and museums in Wyoming feature the Wild West. The Jackson Hole Fall Arts Festival is a 10-day celebration of the fine arts. Thirty galleries host exhibits by local and national artists. The Grand Teton Music Festival is held each summer at Teton Village in Jackson Hole. It features classical music.

Eiji Oue conducts the closing concert of the Grand Teton Music Festival in August 2002.

Books and movies about Wyoming helped the state become well known. In 1902, Owen Wister wrote *The Virginian*. Much of the book is set in the town of Medicine Bow. It was one of the first books written about cowboy life. People now call this type of book a Western. *The Virginian* became a popular Broadway play, a movie, and a TV series. *Rocky IV* was a 1985 boxing movie starring Sylvester Stallone. Parts of it were filmed in Jackson.

Perceptions

Wyoming has wide-open spaces, few people, and an Old West history. It is a state for people who like privacy and the outdoors. Wyomingites want to protect their beautiful natural resources. They do not want ranchers and miners to take away public lands. Some fear that economic growth will spoil their way of life. They enjoy having a low crime rate and small cities.

Candy Trail Mix

Hiking is a popular activity in Yellowstone National Park and Wyoming's three national forests. Trail mixes are quick snacks that provide energy for Wyoming's hikers.

Ingredients

2 cups (480 mL) toasted oat
    cereal
1 cup (240 mL) honey-roasted
    peanuts
1 cup (240 mL) dried apples,
    apricots, or cherries, in small
    pieces
½ cup (120 mL) raisins
1 cup (240 mL) candy-coated
    chocolate pieces

Equipment

Dry-ingredient measuring
    cups
Mixing bowl
Wooden spoon
Airtight container or
    resealable plastic bags

What you do

1. Measure cereal and peanuts into a mixing bowl. Stir with wooden spoon.

2. Measure dried fruit and raisins. Add to bowl and stir.

3. Sprinkle candy-coated chocolate pieces over the mixture and stir again.

4. Store in an airtight container or in resealable plastic bags.

Makes 6 1-cup (240-mL) servings

Wyoming's Flag and Seal

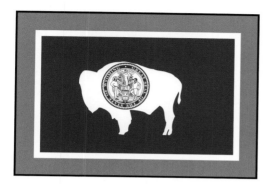

Wyoming's Flag

Wyoming adopted its flag on January 31, 1917. Verna Keyes of Casper designed Wyoming's flag. The red border represents Wyoming's American Indians and the blood of those wounded or killed in battle. The white stripe represents purity and goodness. The blue rectangle on the flag stands for justice. A bison is in the center of the flag. The state seal is on the bison.

Wyoming's State Seal

Images on Wyoming's state seal represent important ideas and the economy in the state. A statue of a woman holds a banner with the state's motto "Equal Rights." Four of Wyoming's major industries, livestock, mines, oil, and grain, are shown on scrolls around pillars. The two men are a rancher and a miner. The shield near the bottom of the seal has the number 44 on it. Wyoming was the 44th state to join the United States. The eagle above the number stands for the United States. There are two years on the seal. In 1869, the territorial government was organized. Wyoming became a state in 1890. Wyoming's state seal was adopted in 1893.

Almanac

General Facts

Nicknames: Cowboy State, Equality State

Population: 493,782 (U.S. Census 2000)
Population rank: 50th

Capital: Cheyenne

Largest cities: Cheyenne, Casper, Laramie, Gillette, Rock Springs

Agriculture

Agricultural products: Beef cattle, wool, alfalfa, sugar beets, wheat, potatoes

Climate

Average winter temperature: 21 degrees Fahrenheit (minus 6 degrees Celsius)

Average summer temperature: 63 degrees Fahrenheit (17 degrees Celsius)

Average annual precipitation: 13 inches (33 centimeters)

Geography

Area: 97,914 square miles (253,597 square kilometers)

Size rank: 10th

Highest point: Gannett Peak, 13,804 feet (4,207 meters) above sea level

Lowest point: Belle Fourche River, 3,100 feet (945 meters) above sea level

Bison

Indian paintbrush

Symbols

Bird: Meadowlark

Dinosaur: Triceratops

Fish: Cutthroat trout

Flower: Indian paintbrush

Fossil: Knightia

Symbols

Gemstone: Jade

Mammal: Bison

Reptile: Horned toad

Song: "Wyoming," by C.E. Winter; music by G.E. Knapp

Tree: Plains cottonwood

Economy

Natural resources: Coal, oil, natural gas, trona, bentonite, uranium

Types of industry: Mining, tourism, farming, ranching, government, transportation

Government

First state governor: Francis Warren, 1890

Statehood: July 10, 1890; 44th state

U.S. Representatives: 1

U.S. Senators: 2

U.S. electoral votes: 3

Counties: 23

Timeline

State History

Around 1800
Shoshone, Crow, Sioux, Cheyenne, and Arapaho people are living in Wyoming.

1812
Robert Stuart discovers South Pass as a way to cross the Rocky Mountains.

1869
Wyoming's territorial government gives Wyoming women the right to vote.

1807
John Colter is the first white man known to explore Wyoming.

1868
The U.S. government creates the Wind River Reservation for the Shoshone. Wyoming becomes a territory.

U.S. History

1775–1783
American colonists fight for their independence from Great Britain in the Revolutionary War.

1620
The Pilgrims establish a colony in North America.

1861–1865
The Civil War is fought between Northern and Southern states.

1890
Wyoming becomes
the 44th state on
July 10.

1925
Wyoming governor Nellie
Tayloe Ross becomes the
first female governor in
the United States.

2001
Former Wyoming
Congressman
Richard Cheney
becomes the vice
president of the
United States.

1958
The nation's first
intercontinental ballistic
missile site is established at
Warren Air Force Base.

1929–1939
The U.S.
economy suffers
during the Great
Depression.

1964
The U.S. Congress
passes the Civil Rights
Act, which makes
discrimination illegal.

1914–1918
World War I is
fought; the United
States enters the war
in 1917.

1939–1945
World War II is
fought; the United
States enters the
war in 1941.

2001
On September 11,
terrorists attack the
World Trade Center
and the Pentagon.

Words to Know

Continental Divide (kon-tuh-NEN-tuhl duh-VIDE)—an imaginary line that splits North America into two parts

geyser (GYE-zur)—an underground spring that shoots hot water through a hole in the ground

intermontane basin (in-tur-MON-tain BAY-suhn)—low, flat land between mountain ranges

refine (ri-FINE)—to clean and make raw materials into finished products

rendezvous (ron-DEH-voo)—a meeting held at a certain time or place; fur traders held rendezvous once a year in the early 1800s.

reservation (rez-ur-VAY-shuhn)—land set aside for use by American Indians

rodeo (ROH-dee-oh)—a contest in which people ride wild horses and rope cattle

trona (TROH-nuh)—a mineral used in making glass products and baking soda

uranium (yu-RAY-nee-uhm)—a silver-white radioactive metal that is the main source of nuclear energy

To Learn More

Baldwin, Guy. *Wyoming.* Celebrate the States. New York: Benchmark Books, 1999.

Boraas, Tracey. *Kit Carson: Mountain Man.* Let Freedom Ring. Mankato, Minn.: Bridgestone Books, 2003.

Jaffe, Elizabeth D. *The Oregon Trail.* Let Freedom Ring. Mankato, Minn.: Bridgestone Books, 2002.

Kent, Deborah. *Wyoming.* America the Beautiful. New York: Children's Press, 2000.

Internet Sites

Do you want to find out more about Wyoming?
Let FactHound, our fact-finding hound dog, do the research for you.

Here's how:
1) Visit ***http://www.facthound.com***
2) Type in the **Book ID** number:
   0736822070
3) Click on **FETCH IT.**

FactHound will fetch Internet sites picked by our editors just for you!

Places to Write and Visit

Buffalo Bill Historical Center
720 Sheridan Avenue
Cody, WY 82414

Office of the Governor
State Capitol Building, Room 124
Cheyenne, WY 82002

Wyoming Business Council
Travel and Tourism Division
214 West 15th Street
Cheyenne, WY 82002

Wyoming Division of State Parks and Historic Sites
Barrett Building
Cheyenne, WY 82002

Wyoming State Museum
Barrett Building
2301 Central Avenue
Cheyenne, WY 82002

Yellowstone National Park
P.O. Box 168
Yellowstone National Park, WY 82190-0168

The canyon of the Yellowstone River is part of Yellowstone National Park.

Index

T 57087